WRITING A
RESEARCH PAPER

VALERIE BODDEN | ILLUSTRATIONS BY NATE WILLIAMS

CREATIVE ✿ EDUCATION

Published by Creative Education
P.O. Box 227, Mankato, Minnesota 56002
Creative Education is an imprint of The Creative Company
www.thecreativecompany.us

Design and production by Liddy Walseth
Art direction by Rita Marshall
Printed in the United States of America

Illustrations by Nate Williams © 2014

Library of Congress Cataloging-in-Publication Data
Bodden, Valerie.
Writing a research paper / Valerie Bodden.
p. cm. — (Classroom how-to)
Includes bibliographical references and index.
Summary: An approachable guide to help master and apply the
writing, speaking, and listening skills involved in conducting
research projects, composing arguments, and conveying results.
ISBN 978-1-60818-283-1
1. Report writing—Juvenile literature. 2. Research—Juvenile literature. I. Title.
LB1047.3.B64 2014
371.30281—dc23   2013029622

CCSS: RI.5.1, 2, 3, 7, 8, 9; RH.6-8.1, 6, 9; W.5.1, 2, 3, 4, 5, 7, 8, 9, 10;
W.6.1, 2, 4, 7, 8, 9; SL.6.1, 3, 4, 6

First Edition
2 4 6 8 9 7 5 3 1

TABLE OF CONTENTS

HOMEWORK. *Tests.* Speeches. **Papers.**

Does it sometimes feel like you face an endless list of tasks to complete for school? And why? To make your teachers happy? Well, yes, completing your work is likely to make your teachers happy. But that is not the only reason teachers assign work. Believe it or not, writing papers, taking tests, and making speeches benefits you, too. Every time you complete one of these tasks, you learn something more about how to do it, and you become more prepared to do it again in the future—in high school, college, and even possibly your career. But more than that, these tasks teach you how to learn, how to study, how to find information, and how to present your viewpoint. And such skills will help you not only in the classroom but also in life.

Research papers, for example, can teach you how to find information.

And that's a skill that will be useful in nearly every aspect of your life—from

researching the best price on a product to looking up how to design your own

bird feeder. Of course, just as with any new task, it takes information and time

to master the research paper.

How do you know when you

need to do research? Where

do you find that research?

And how do you organize

and incorporate it into your

paper? Learning the answers

to these questions will help

you write a research paper

that will make your teacher

happy—and teach you some-

thing in the process!

CHAPTER
ONE

RESEARCH PAPER
PERKS & PITFALLS

If you've never written a research paper before, you may still be wondering exactly what one is and how it differs from a "regular," non-research paper. Well, in a non-research paper, you write about your own thoughts and ideas. If your teacher asks for a paper about what you did on your summer vacation, for example, you don't need to do research. You were there, you lived it, and you can tell about it based on your own memories and feelings.

A research paper, on the other hand, combines your thoughts and ideas with research gleaned from other sources. That research might be in the form of facts and figures, expert opinions, historical accounts, or even survey results. If, for example, your teacher wants you to expand your summer vacation paper into a research paper, you might research and write about the history of Disney World (if you were lucky enough to travel there). Or, you might write a paper focusing on education experts who favor eliminating summer vacation and holding school year-round. What about a paper about summer employment among middle and high school students? Chances are, you don't have all the information you need to write about any of these topics stored in your head. So you would have to conduct research.

That might sound hard, but it isn't. After all, you probably do research every day without even realizing it. When you want to know about the latest styles, you flip open a magazine. If you want to find the best price on a new video game, you comparison shop online. And if you want to check the weather, you turn on the TV or go to a website.

So if you already know how to research, why does your teacher want you to write a whole paper based on

INFORMATION

research? You know what they say: practice makes perfect. Writing a research paper can help you figure out when and where to look for information—and knowing when you need information and where to find it is one of the most important steps in learning how to learn. Representing a range of topics, research papers can introduce you to a whole host of information sources, from encyclopedias and books in libraries to online newspapers and databases.

In addition to teaching you how to find information, writing a research paper can help you learn how to interpret, analyze, and evaluate that information. As you research, you'll come to

"KNOWLEDGE IS OF TWO KINDS. WE KNOW A SUBJECT OURSELVES, OR WE KNOW WHERE WE CAN FIND INFORMATION UPON IT."

— James Boswell

realize that not all sources are equally reliable—and you'll learn to identify those that are more authoritative. In addition, you'll learn to use others' ideas to shape your own thoughts so that you can develop informed opinions.

Of course, learning to conduct research, analyze information, and form opinions are all skills that will benefit you as you continue through school. But the ability to write a research paper is key in many careers as well. Lawyers, journalists, teachers, engineers, and others all need to be able to utilize information learned from other sources in a meaningful way.

Writing a research paper is not simply an exercise in learning to research or a step toward getting your dream job, though. Research papers also serve a more immediate purpose. They can inform or **persuade** your reader, investigate a problem, or analyze a subject. A research paper about George Washington's life, for example, would likely take an informative tone, while one that tries to convince readers to vote for healthier school lunches would make use of arguments and persuasion. A research paper could also investigate the causes of local water pollution or analyze the use of light and dark imagery in C. S. Lewis's

The Lion, the Witch, and the Wardrobe. In each of these cases, the paper has a specific purpose and will need to use sources that support that purpose. At the same time, research papers provide you, the writer, with yet another benefit: you get to learn a whole lot about a topic that interests you (so be sure to pick a topic that actually *does* interest you—but more on that later).

Even with all the benefits of writing a research paper, it's only fair to admit that there are some challenges involved in the process. One of the hardest steps for many students is picking a topic worth researching. You need to find a subject that is neither too broad nor too narrow—one that enough has been written about to provide you with

sources but that also isn't so common that everyone already knows everything there is to know about it.

Once you've picked a topic, you might be intimidated by the mere idea of having to research it. Where do you start? How many sources do you need? How do you choose which sources to use? How do you know when you have enough information? Although there are no hard and fast answers to many of these questions, there are several guidelines that can make the research process less stressful.

Finally, once you have completed your research, what do you do with it? How do you put it all together? Writing a research paper involves learning to carefully integrate research with your own thoughts and ideas. In other words, you need to figure out how to use your sources to prove a point of your own rather than simply creating a catalog of information you have discovered.

33

INTEGRATE RESEARCH

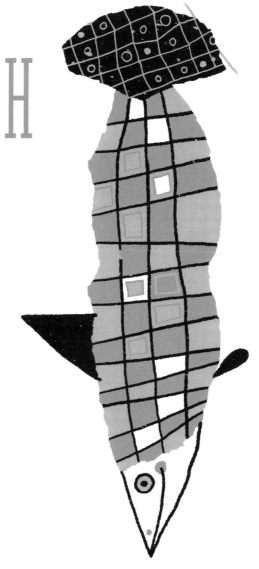

One final challenge remains: research papers require that you cite the sources of your information. This means that whenever you use an idea that is not your own, you need to give credit to the author of that idea, usually by including her last name and the page number of the work from which you took the information. Citing sources may take some getting used to at first, but the good news is that the more you practice it (by citing more sources, of course), the more natural it will become!

PUTTING THE RESEARCH IN THE RESEARCH PAPER

Before you can even begin conducting research for your paper, you have to figure out what it is that you want to research. In some cases, your teacher may not give you a choice. If he tells you to write a research paper about how a bill becomes a law, then that's what you'll write about. But teachers often leave the choice of subject—or at least some part of it—to their students. Sometimes, they give you the freedom to choose a specific topic within a general subject area, such as science or literature. Or your teacher may ask you to write a paper about some aspect of pollution, another broad issue.

In some cases, your teacher might leave the choice of topic completely up to you. While this may seem like the ideal situation, it can cause some students to panic. After all, if you can write about *anything*, how do you go about choosing *which* anything to focus on? If you feel that way, don't worry. There are plenty of ways to find a topic worth writing about. The most important advice here is to choose something you are interested in. Writing a research paper is time-consuming.

HOW DO YOU KNOW WHAT YOU ARE INTERESTED IN?

X-RAY

MiLK

You don't want to be stuck raking through piles of information about a subject that puts you to sleep.

But how do you know what you're interested in? Chances are that's easier to figure out than you think. You can brainstorm ideas. Just sit down and make a list of any and every topic that comes into your head, from the silly (maybe clown college) to the scary (how about haunted houses?). When you are done, go through your list. Does any topic jump out at you? If that doesn't work, you might try a more deliberate exercise. First, think about all the people who interest you and make

a list. Then list all the activities you enjoy. Make another list of places or events you'd like to know more about. Now look through your lists. Are any of your interests strong enough to serve as the topic for a research paper? If you're really stuck for ideas, you might try browsing the Internet or wandering through the stacks at the library. You never know—something may catch your interest.

Whether your teacher chooses the general subject area or leaves the decision to you, you need to make sure not only that your topic will interest you but also that it will be possible to write about it. True, you can probably write something about nearly any subject, but this is a research paper, which means that you need to be able to find enough—but not too much—research about your topic. You're probably not going to be able to find any books or articles about your neighbor's habit of saying "howdy" instead of "hello," for example. Your topic is too narrow in this case. But if you broaden your focus to regional sayings, you might just have a researchable topic on your hands.

If, on the other hand, you decide that you are interested in the American Civil War, you will soon find that

your topic is too broad, with thousands of sources available. In this case, you need to narrow your subject, focusing on just one aspect of the Civil War. Ask yourself what it is about the Civil War that interests you. Do you want to know more about how it divided families? Are you interested in how African Americans were treated in the North or South during or after the war? Or do you want to research battlefield injuries?

One way to figure out if your topic is too broad or too narrow is to conduct a **preliminary** search for sources. Start with your library's online book catalog. Type in your topic and see how many sources come up. If there

are more than 10 or 20, your topic is probably too broad. If there are only one or two, you may have picked a topic that is too narrow to have been written about in much detail.

While a preliminary search can clue you in to a topic that is too broad, it can also actually help you to narrow that topic. Look through your search results. Do any of them cover specific aspects of your general topic? Another great place to find ideas for narrowing your topic is an encyclopedia. Most encyclopedias break large subject areas down into smaller parts. Skim the encyclopedia entry for your subject to see if any of its subheadings jump out at you.

As you conduct your preliminary research, don't be afraid to reshape your topic—or to change it altogether. But, by the time you've completed your preliminary research, you will want to have a pretty good idea of what your specific topic will be. Otherwise, as you move on to more in-depth research, you won't know exactly what you're looking for, and you may waste a lot of time sorting through **irrelevant** material.

Once you know what you need, you can head to your library or log on to your library's website and start digging! Often, the best place to begin is

with a reference work such as an encyclopedia. Encyclopedias can give you a clear overview of your subject—and their **bibliographies** can lead you to further sources. Once you have a general grasp on your subject, you can turn to books, magazines, and **journal** articles for more detailed information. You'll probably have to go to the library for access to most books. But most libraries allow you to read magazine, newspaper, and journal articles through online **databases**. If you need more information on how to access such databases, just talk to your librarian—that's what he's there for. Depending on your subject, you might also look for non-print sources, such as audio and video recordings.

The Internet can be another good source of information on many topics—especially current issues that may not yet have been covered by print sources. Of course, just because information appears on a website does not mean that it is accurate. You need to carefully evaluate any information you take from the Internet. Certain sites are more trustworthy than others. The sites of prominent newspapers such as *The New York Times*, for example, tend to be reliable, as do most government sites (with **domains** ending in .gov) and many educational sites (domains ending in .edu).

As you evaluate what you read on a website, consider the site's author (if listed), its publisher (for example, is it a business that has something to gain through its claims?), the date the information was updated, and whether the author has cited the sources of his or her information. And be sure to cross-check the information you find with another reliable source.

While it is especially important to evaluate the accuracy of Internet sources, this does not mean that if something is printed in a book or article it is automatically true, either. You need to evaluate these sources in much the same way as you do Internet sources. Is the author an expert on the subject (check if his **credentials** are listed)? Is the publisher reputable (such as a university press or a scholarly journal)? Is the book current? (This is generally more important for topics in fields such as science and technology than in literature or history.) Does the author cite his sources?

Most teachers require you to use a variety of sources and source types in your research. And just when you think you have the difference between journal articles, magazines, encyclopedias, and books down, your teacher may also say that you need to use both primary and secondary sources. In simpler terms, all he's saying is that he wants you to use both firsthand and secondhand accounts in your research. A primary source is a firsthand account, written by a person who experienced an event. An autobiography, for example, is a primary source. So is a newspaper article narrating a current event. For example, articles about the first moon walk, written at the time of the moon walk, are primary sources. If you are writing about a particular literary work, that work is a primary source. Field research, such as an experiment or a survey, is also primary research, as is the original report that details such research. Secondary research, on the other hand, gives a secondhand account of a topic; it analyzes or interprets a primary source. So a biography is a secondary source, as is a newspaper article analyzing an event of the past. Articles about a literary work are also secondary sources. Chances are that as you search out sources, you will naturally find both primary and secondary sources, but if one seems hard to come by, you might have to dig a bit deeper. What you find will likely be worth the effort—it may just contain that gem of information you've been looking for!

"RESEARCH IS FORMALIZED CURIOSITY. IT IS POKING AND PRYING WITH A PURPOSE."

— Zora Neale Hurston

CHAPTER THREE

IT'S ALL IN THE NOTES

As you sort through the research you've collected, think about what kinds of information you need to support your topic. Are you going to rely on facts and figures, **anecdotes**, expert opinions—or maybe a combination of all three? Knowing the types of information you need will help you to recognize useful sources—and to set aside those that won't help make your point.

Whenever you identify a source that appears to hold useful information, you should make note of its publication information in a work-ing bibliography. The term "working bibliography" might sound daunting, but it is simply a list of sources from which you have taken information that you might use in your final paper. For books, the working bibliography should include the author's name, the title, the city and state of publication, the publisher's name, and the year copyrighted. Articles from periodicals require similar information: author's name, article title, periodical title, date published, and page number of arti-cle. For Internet sources, write down as much information as you can find,

MAKE SURE TO START EARLY

including the author's name, sponsoring organization, date updated, Web address, and the date you accessed the information. Keeping track of this information now will save a lot of time later when you are ready to assemble your final bibliography. In fact, you can even format your working bibliography according to your teacher's requirements now so that you don't have to reformat your entries later. (For more about the different ways to format bibliography entries, see the next chapter.)

Of course, you need to keep track of not only which sources you use but also the information each provides. That's where note-taking comes in. This step will probably take up the bulk of the time you spend on your research paper, so make sure to start early. Different writers prefer different techniques for note-taking. As long as your teacher doesn't require you to follow a specific format, feel free to choose the one that works best for you (or even to create your own system).

Long ago, in the days before computers, many people chose to take notes on index cards, and some people still use this system today. The idea is to write one note per card. At the bottom, note which source the information is from. (You don't have to list the entire source—usually just the author's last name and the page number will do.) At the top of each card, write a word or two that describes the topic of the note. For example, if you are researching ways to protect wildlife, you might head some index cards "wild-life refuges" and others "laws and regulations." When you've finished taking notes, you'll be able to easily organize your cards by topic.

If you don't want to worry about holding on to a stack of index cards, you might instead choose to create a research notebook. In this case, you might keep a separate page for notes from each source. Or you could make notes about each subheading related to your topic on a separate page. Just be sure to somehow record which source each note is from—by placing the author's last name and the page number before or after the note, for example.

If the idea of writing notes by hand makes you cringe, you can use a computer to take notes instead. You might keep separate pages or files for notes from each source. Or you might prefer to organize your notes by topic, with separate pages or files for each

(again, being sure to indicate which source each note comes from). One of the advantages of using a computer to take notes is that when it comes time to organize your information, you can simply copy and paste your notes into your outline.

Whatever method you choose for note-taking, there are three types of notes that you will take: summary, paraphrase, and quotation. Summary notes do exactly what they say: they summarize what you have read. If you simply want to make note of an author's general ideas but don't feel that you need to use any of the specific details she offers, you could simply write a brief summary of her thoughts on the subject. For example: "This author supports raising the driving age

to 18, in the belief that teens are not old enough to handle the responsibilities of driving until they are officially considered 'adults.'"

When you paraphrase, on the other hand, you restate an author's ideas in your own words. Rather than summarizing the general content of an article or book, a paraphrase notes the specific content of a phrase, sentence, or even paragraph. As you para-

phrase, it is important not to copy the author's words exactly (that's where quotations come in) or even too closely—you don't want to unintentionally **plagiarize**. The benefit of careful paraphrasing now is that when it comes time to write your paper, you can plug your paraphrases right into it—you've already done the hard part of writing them.

Finally, in some instances, you will want to make note of an author's exact words. You might quote a source if she says something particularly well—better than you could restate it. Or you might quote an acknowledged expert in the field to give your paper **credibility**. In some cases, you might also quote a source that disagrees with you. That way, you can be sure that you are stating that author's argument accurately, without introducing your own bias. As you make note of quotes, be sure to do so carefully. Double-check that you've gotten the source's words exactly as they appear in the original. And be sure not to take a quote out of context. If a source says, "I support medicinal marijuana use in the most extreme cases," it would be inaccurate to present only the segment "I support medicinal marijuana use." Such a quote does

QUOTE THE SOURCE

29

PERSUADE YOUR READER TO TAKE ACTION

not honestly reflect the source's true views on the subject. Most importantly, be sure to enclose your quoted material in quotation marks so that you don't later think that you've come up with these words on your own.

By the time you have finished taking notes, you might feel overwhelmed by all the information you have collected. How are you ever going to make a paper out of this mess? Now it's time to organize—and that is usually accomplished with an outline. Many teachers require students to turn in an outline as part of the research paper process. But even if yours doesn't, an outline can be a useful tool in helping you get a grip on all the information you've collected. A formal outline uses a combination of roman numerals (such as I, V, and X), letters, and arabic numerals, like this:

I. Reasons for increasing obesity rate
   A. Less activity
      1. Computers, video games, television use
      2. Desk jobs vs. physical labor
   B. Changing eating habits
      1. Processed foods
      2. Fast food
   C. Environment
      1. Lack of sidewalks
      2. Distance between destinations
         discourages walking or biking
      3. Prevalence of elevators and escalators
   D. Genes

In such an outline, the roman numeral represents the topic of a paragraph. The letters represent subtopics, and the arabic numerals list points to be made under each subtopic. If your teacher requires that you hand in an outline, she will likely specify whether short phrases will do or if she prefers full sentences for each point. If you are not required to hand in an outline, you can format it however you like. Perhaps you simply want to make a list of all the topics you'll cover and in what order. Or maybe you want to be more detailed, noting where you'll make use of specific sources and quotes.

As you outline, you need to consider how best to organize your information. You want your paper to flow naturally and logically from one point to another. If your topic is historical or discusses a specific process, you might choose to arrange your paper chronologically. If, on the other hand, you are trying to persuade your reader to take action on an issue, you might organize your arguments from weakest to strongest or vice versa. Or, if you want to discuss two ideas or concepts,

"IN ORDER TO WIDEN ONE'S KNOWLEDGE AND EXPERIENCE, ONE MUST LISTEN TO THE WORDS OF OTHERS, READ BOOKS, AND FORM ONE'S OWN IDEAS."

— *Yukichi Fukuzawa*

you might compare and contrast them. If you are analyzing a problem, you might talk about cause and effect, or you could define the problem and then discuss a solution.

By the time you are done outlining—or possibly even sooner—you should be able to write your thesis statement. This is usually a single sentence that states the main argument of your paper and clues readers in to what is coming. Try to be as specific as possible in your thesis. For example, trying to employ "Twitter use has really taken off" as a thesis would be too vague. A more specific thesis, targeted to the point of the paper, might be that "Twitter use has soared as people use the service to connect with friends, follow pop culture, and market products." Such a specific thesis will guide the development of your paper and make the next step—writing—all the easier!

CHAPTER FOUR

PUTTING IT ALL TOGETHER

With your outline at your side, writing your first draft should go fairly smoothly. You already know what you want to write and in what order you want to write it—so all you have to do is get it down on paper. Like any essay, a research paper has three main parts: the introduction, the body, and the conclusion. The introduction of your paper needs to get your readers' attention. This doesn't mean that the introduction has to be flashy—but it does need to be interesting. You might start with an anecdote, a particularly apt quote, or a shocking fact or statistic. For example, a paper about cheating in school might begin: "Everybody does it. In fact, 95 percent of high school students say they've cheated at least once." The introduction should also let readers know why your topic is important. In some cases, the introduction might need to provide some background information as well. If you are writing about a book, for example, you might include a brief summary of the action. Most importantly, the introduction needs to let readers know the point of your paper— your thesis. The thesis statement can appear anywhere in the introduction, but most writers find that it fits most naturally at the end of the paragraph.

The body of the paper is where you prove your point. It usually consists of three or more paragraphs, each covering a different aspect of your subject. Each paragraph should include a topic sentence. This sentence lets readers know what the paragraph is about. The rest of the paragraph supports the topic sentence. For example, in the case of the cheating paper, your topic sentence might be, "Although the old saying states that 'cheaters never win,' in many cases this seems not to hold true." Then, you might go on to offer figures about the percentage of cheating that goes undetected. Or you might include a story about a student who received an award based on grades attained by cheating.

The conclusion follows the body of your paper, and it does just what it says it does—it brings your paper to a close. At this point, you want to remind readers of your findings by briefly summarizing your main points and restating your thesis. You might also tell readers what this information means to them or why it matters. Like the introduction and the body, the conclusion can include anecdotes,

facts, or quotes. In the end, the goal of the conclusion is to leave a lasting impression in your reader's mind.

Since this is a research paper, you will obviously need to include your research in it. This does not mean, however, that your paper should simply be sentence after sentence of facts, quotes, and stories from your sources. You need to include your own thoughts in the paper as well. Your sources simply help to support those thoughts. As you incorporate research into your paper, strive to include a combination of summaries, paraphrases, and quotes.

There's one more thing to keep in mind as you weave your sources into your paper: you need to cite those sources. Why? Well, for one thing, citing a source gives credit where credit is due. Researchers over the decades—or even centuries—have worked hard to understand your topic, and their work should be acknowledged. In fact, if you fail to credit your sources, you are committing plagiarism. In many cases, plagiarism is grounds for a failing grade or worse. So any time you include a thought that isn't your own, whether it is in the form of a quote, paraphrase, or summary, be sure to let readers know whose it is (and if you are quoting a source, be sure to enclose the quote in quotation marks). At the same time, keep in mind that you don't have to cite what is known as "common knowledge." In other words, if a fact is already well known (such as that George Washington was the first president of the United States), you don't need to credit a source.

"READING FURNISHES THE MIND ONLY WITH MATERIAL FOR KNOWLEDGE; IT IS THINKING THAT MAKES WHAT WE READ OURS."

— John Locke

TRUST WHAT YOU HAVE TO SAY

Beyond avoiding plagiarism, citing your sources gives your paper credibility. If readers don't know where you found your information, they may as well believe that you made it up. But if they can **verify** your research by checking it against your sources, they know they can trust what you have to say.

Different fields of study use different formats for citing sources. English and humanities classes generally follow guidelines established by the Modern Language Association (MLA), while papers written for the social sciences often follow the American Psychological Association's (APA) style guidelines. Your teacher will likely specify which of these styles (or another) you should use and provide detailed instructions on how to use it.

There are also many handbooks that cover the ins and outs of the different citation formats.

Although each citation style has its own rules, the goal of each is to help readers find exactly where you got your information. To this end, most citation styles require that you provide the author's last name as well as the page number from which you took the information. (In some cases, the year a work was published is also included.) With this information, your reader can flip to your bibliography and find the entry with that author's name. That entry will tell the reader the name of the source and when and where it was published. Then all he has to do is find a copy of that source at his local library or online and flip to the page you've indicated—and voilà: he's found exactly the information you said he would find.

Some style guidelines require the use of **footnotes** for citations, but both the MLA and APA rely on parenthetical in-text citations. Sound complicated? Not really. All this means is that your citation is included in parentheses, usually at the end of the sentence in which you have incorporated information from a source. The period for your sentence goes outside the final parenthesis of the citation.

In MLA style, the parenthetical citation includes the author's last name and the page number. For example, to cite this page of this book in MLA style, you would write "(Bodden 41)." In APA style, the citation would be slightly different and would include the year of publication as well as punctuation marks and the abbreviation "p." for the word *page*: "(Bodden, 2015, p. 41)." If, however, you mention the author's last name in your sentence (for example, "According to Bodden,...."), you can

HOWEVER ALSO BESIDES

leave it out of the citation and just include the page number (or the year and page number for APA style) in parentheses.

Once you have finished your first draft, complete with all the necessary citations, you may think that your work is done. Not quite! Now it's time to **revise** your paper. Go back and read what you've written. If any of your paragraphs seems weak, add to them. And, if you find information that just doesn't seem to fit, cut it. As tempting as it might be to make use of all your research (after all, you worked hard to dig it up), it can actually weaken your paper to include irrelevant information. As you read, consider whether your paper flows well from one thought to another. If not, add **transitions**, such as "also," "however," or "besides." Finally, be sure to proofread for spelling or grammatical errors.

Okay, now that you've revised your paper, you're done, right? Almost. Just one more detail to cover: remember that bibliography (also sometimes called a works cited list) that we talked about earlier? Well, now's the time to put it together. Fortunately, you already have your working bibliography, so all you have to do is figure out which sources you didn't use for your paper and delete them from your list. Then make sure your entries are formatted correctly according to the style your teacher requires. In MLA style, for example, entries for books are formatted like this: Bodden, Valerie. *Writing a Research Paper*. Mankato: Creative Education, 2015. Print.

In APA style, the citation includes much of the same information, but in a different order: Bodden, V. (2015). *Writing a Research Paper.* Mankato, MN: Creative Education.

To learn more about the formatting requirements for other types of sources, such as magazine and newspaper articles, DVDs, or Internet sites, consult your teacher, an Internet style guide such as the Purdue Online Writing Lab (http://owl.english.purdue .edu/owl/resource/747/01/), or a stylebook such as the *MLA Handbook for Writers of Research Papers* (available at any library).

And *now*, your paper is done. You

TIME TO PUT IT TOGETHER

FORM YOUR OWN THOUGHTS

can take pride in the fact that you've worked hard to collect and organize research and to form your own thoughts about your subject—and then to incorporate both into a well-written paper that would make any teacher smile. And it should make you smile, too; after all, you've learned a new set of skills that you'll be able to make use of for the rest of your life!

GLOSSARY

anecdotes: brief stories recounting a specific incident or event

bibliographies: lists of sources (such as books, articles, and websites) consulted in the course of writing a research paper, article, or book

cite: to quote someone else's work as evidence for an idea or argument

credentials: a list of qualifications (such as degrees earned or awards received) that reflects a person's area of expertise

credibility: the quality of being believable

databases: organized collections of data, or information, stored on a computer

domains: the names of sites on the Internet

footnotes: notes printed at the bottom of a page to provide additional information or references to sources of information found in the text

irrelevant: unrelated to the subject

journal: a publication, often scholarly in nature, that typically contains articles related to a specific field of study

persuade: to try to convince someone to believe or do something

plagiarize: to take credit for another person's thoughts or words

preliminary: something that is done in preparation for something else

revise: to rewrite for the purpose of improving

transitions: words or phrases that connect one idea to another

verify: to check that something is true or accurate

SELECTED BIBLIOGRAPHY

Ballenger, Bruce. *The Curious Researcher: A Guide to Writing Research Papers*. 7th ed. New York: Pearson Education, 2011.

Book Builders LLC. *How to Write a Great Research Paper*. Hoboken, N.J.: J. Wiley & Sons, 2004.

Ellis, Dave. *Becoming a Master Student*. 14th ed. Belmont, Calif.: Cengage Learning, 2011.

Gibaldi, Joseph. *MLA Handbook for Writers of Research Papers*. 7th ed. New York: Modern Language Association of America, 2009.

Lester, James D. Jr., and James D. Lester Sr. *Research Paper Handbook: Your Complete Guide*. 3rd ed. Tucson: Good Year Books, 2005.

Purdue University. "Purdue Online Writing Lab." The Purdue OWL. http://owl.english.purdue.edu/owl.

Sullivan, Helen, and Linda Sernoff. *Research Reports: A Guide for Middle and High School Students*. Brookfield, Conn.: Millbrook Press, 1996.

Turabian, Kate L. *A Manual for Writers of Research Papers, Theses, and Dissertations: Chicago Style for Students and Researchers*. 7th ed. Chicago: University of Chicago Press, 2007.

READ MORE

Bankhead, Elizabeth, Janet Nichols, and Dawn Vaughn. *Write It!: A Guide for Research*. 3rd ed. Westport, Conn.: Libraries Unlimited, 2009.

Book Builders LLC. *How to Write a Great Research Paper*. Hoboken, N.J.: J. Wiley & Sons, 2004.

Jensen, Eric. *Student Success Secrets*. 5th ed. Hauppauge, N.Y.: Barron's, 2003.

Toronto Public Library. *Research Ate My Brain: The Panic-Proof Guide to Surviving Homework*. Toronto: Annick Press, 2005.

WEBSITES

Duke University: Citing Sources and Avoiding Plagiarism
http://library.duke.edu/research/plagiarism/
Watch a video of Duke University students talking about the difficulties—and importance—of citing sources.

Internet Public Library: A+ Research & Writing
http://www.ipl.org/div/aplus/
This site offers a step-by-step guide to the research process.

KidsHealth: What Is Plagiarism?
http://kidshealth.org/kid/feeling/school/plagiarism.html
Learn more about plagiarism and how to avoid committing it.

Note: Every effort has been made to ensure that the websites listed above are suitable for children, that they have educational value, and that they contain no inappropriate material. However, because of the nature of the Internet, it is impossible to guarantee that these sites will remain active indefinitely or that their contents will not be altered.

INDEX